STEELY DAN
two against nature

Piano/Vocal arrangements by David Pearl, John Ferguson, and Marc Irwin
Cover photography by Michael Northrop

ISBN 1-57560-374-8

Visit our website at www.cherrylane.com

Photo by Frank Ocker

3

contents

Interview with

Donald Fagen and Walter Becker

By Davin Seay

4

On Two Against Nature, *Steely Dan's brilliant new Giant Records release, Donald Fagen and Walter Becker return to the studio for the first time since 1979's multi-platinum album* Gaucho *with a collection of new originals and an all-star cast of supporting players. The result: a quintessential musical blend that consolidates Steely Dan's reputation as one of the most innovative and original songwriting and producing teams of all time.*

With its trademark synthesis of rock and jazz, Two Against Nature *continues a tradition that began with such landmark hits as "Do It Again" and "Rikki Don't Lose That Number" and continued through "Peg," "Hey Nineteen," and many more. Now, after 20 years, Steely Dan picks up where they left off with standout tracks such as "Gaslighting Abbie" "Cousin Dupree," and "What a Shame About Me." It's most definitely been worth the wait.*

5

Walter: We had been talking about the idea of doing this for a while. We had written songs together, a couple of different times since *Gaucho*. There was a time in the middle '80s when we got together and wrote some tunes and then we worked on at least one tune for Donald's record. So we had in the back of our minds the idea that we had some songs and some ideas for a new album. I guess after the last tour in '96 we decided: *well, let's go and do it if we're going to do it.* That's when we started.

Donald: I think there were a couple of songs that may date back to the '80s—at least the germinal ideas of them. But most of the songs were written in the '90s.

Walter: It's always been our habit in writing to look at pieces that we've had lying around for years or to rewrite songs that we perhaps finished and decided weren't that good. But all of the lyrics and all of the finished song structures, melodies, and so on, are really new.

Donald: I think when we get together we just end up with a certain style, which hopefully has evolved over the years. I don't think we were really remembering what we used to do in the '70s or '80s, really. It was just a matter of collecting some fragments that we had worked on either alone or together and seeing if we could come up with some music that was interesting enough so that we would actually want to make records out of the material.

Walter: I think we actually started recording in November of '97.

Donald: There were times in between when we went back to write some more or took off.

Walter: I remember we took that weekend off.

Donald: That weekend . . . went down to Tijuana.

Walter: It was a long weekend—Friday, Saturday, Sunday.

Donald: This material is all pretty new. As I say, some of the things may be based on ideas from many years ago that we had on tape, which is usually a cassette and a boom box— old work tapes that we sort of collate once in a while. It's a renewable process because obviously some things don't work out the way you want; so you end up with these fragments that can be used later for something else, if it comes along. For instance, if you're writing a song and a chord progression leads to a spot you know sounds familiar, it will turn out to be similar to a chord progression from some fragment that we never used. We say, *this effect might sound good here*, so we'll use that and we'll just kick those things out. You end up sewing everything together in a way, and I think most things are so much more random than they seem. Then when you put them together, hopefully they won't seem random.

Walter: Yeah, it's true. It's surprising when you're writing stuff how many different ways a thing could work and still sound right. A lot of times we'll sit there trying to figure out which is best, and they all sound pretty good.

Donald: What it is, is you'll be writing something and realize the section you're about to write you've already written for a song that never matured. For instance, "West of Hollywood" has a chorus where we started playing something, and it reminded us of a chorus of a sort of reggae song we wrote in the '80s. So we dug it up and we adapted it. We had to change a few things, but essentially we were able to use that idea 15 years later.

Walter: We're very economical. We like to use old little scraps of things that we find.

Donald: In "West of Hollywood" we were trying to write a love story really, but reducing it to the main points, almost telling it from a theoretical thing, like from an outline someone would make for a screenplay or something.

Walter: Yeah, and I think in a way it was as far as the lyrics went. It was a very stylistic exercise trying to come up with a narrative mode that was different than what we usually do or what people usually do in songs.

Donald: It occurs to me now it was sort of like when someone is trying to tell you something about some extreme experience and being carried away, by a love affair or whatever, and there seems to be no language to communicate it to someone else. We were trying—what language would you use?

Walter: Right. And the other thing is that you can imagine some sort of transforming experience that leads you off in a place where you're no longer really able to offer a coherent account of how you got there. All you can do is allude to various stations along the way that you stopped at, and it doesn't really make sense.

Donald: It's like a really incoherent person trying to tell a really serious story.

Walter: Right. And you know, it's sort of typical post-modern fashion that the narrative mode or voice sort of overwhelms the actual narrative a little bit.

Donald: The style almost takes over.

Walter: Right. Most of the playing that's done on the record is done by guys that are right here in New York. So we sort of knew where we were going to start and figured we'd see—as has always been the case in the past—see what we'd get. If you try to cut a track with a particular band and it's not successful, often that gives you some idea of either how the concept of the track or the arrangement has to change to make it successful or how the instrumentation or the actual personnel might change.

Donald: Or in some cases we used a drum track or a bass track and did the rest of the playing ourselves on guitar and keyboards— because it just demanded a certain feel that may have been there in the drum track but not in the other parts. On "West of Hollywood" we had a solo section that we wanted Chris Potter to play on saxophone. But it turned out to be a guitar solo. But during the course of the day when he came in, he said, "Let me take a shot at the tag," which he had heard, and he tried it . . . and actually I think he said, "Let me take this home for a couple of days and look at it," because it was quite complex. Then he came in a couple of days later and just did a couple of takes. We didn't actually plan on having a saxophone solo there. I think we didn't know what was going to go there. We had the chord progression; at one point it was just going to be something almost baroque-sounding. But he played it so well that we realized that we should keep it. It was completely improvisational. Some tracks were live and some were sort of cyber-live. In some cases we used part of a drum track and we made it a loop section or something. We do that. But essentially it was played with a band, just like the old days.

Walter: Back in the '70s we were basically working with 24-track machines and there was a space limitation for layering tracks that doesn't exist anymore. So we probably ended up with more layers of interwoven separate tracks. I think also the way we ended up doing overdubs on some of these tunes and defining the tunes with sort of fragmentary parts and then adding more parts to them means there's more tracks of guitars.

Donald: I think Walter is more confident about soloing this time around so he does really all the guitar solos. It makes it stylistically more unified too. Rather than having two or three guitar players in showcase, it's essentially just Walter playing.

Walter: I only have one chop.

Donald: But that one chop is in very good condition.

Walter: Horn charts were written after most of the stuff was done on the tracks.

Donald: I used to [write horn parts] in the '70s. Usually I used to do them or Walter and I used to do them, usually in conjunction with one of the musicians—somebody who would help us with some of the technical parts. I've just become a little more confident about writing the parts and sort of hand them off to somebody to copy. Then I got a lot of help this time from a guy named Michael Linhardt, who is a trumpet player, who played trumpet on the dates and also helped with the arrangements. If we feel it needs some support from horns or some sparkle, we'll write a horn chart for it.

Walter: Minimal as they may be.

Donald: That's usually something we do last. "Jack of Speed" is really just about when one member of a couple starts to lose it in some way. The most obvious question is, Are you talking about actual speed, like the drug "speed"? It's really not that; it has to do with sort of manic stages people get into for one reason or another. The cautionary smile. He's out there; he is living too large.

Walter: I think for the most part these are not particular people that we know. Rather than that, they're either exaggerations of our own experiences or products of our own imaginations or fantasies.

Donald: Or based on people we know, maybe, but no one specific. Maybe combinations of things you hear—or just trying to isolate some impulse that someone our age might have. Not necessarily us, but someone. "Gaslighting" had its origin in the classic film *Gaslight*. To "gaslight" is what Charles Boyer did to Ingrid Bergman. He tried to convince her that she was insane by moving things around in the house.

Walter: Constantly turning the lights lower and lower.

Donald: It's about a guy who, along with his secret lover, is essentially trying to get rid of his wife or drive her insane. They steal her clothes. They get 15-watt light bulbs and put them in place of the usual light bulbs so it looks really dark in the house. It's very menacing.

Walter: It was sort of meant to be harmonically the effect of a knife between the ribs there.

Donald: It's sort of like the aural equivalent of an Alfred Hitchcock movie.

Walter: We have a very antique idea of what modernity is, I guess.

Donald: When we started, modern was Boyd Rayburn and his orchestra, which seemed pretty modern to us.

Walter: It seems to us that since we were fortunate enough to have a going career for as many years as we did in the '70s, making records, and still today touring and doing other stuff, that there is an audience for what we like and what we've been doing right along. And so we sort of assume that there is, without actually checking to see how it might fit in with the context of things that other people are doing. Because the truth is, even back in 1971, what we were doing didn't really relate that strongly to what other people were doing. Basically people are creating something that's going to fit the mood of the moment or the style of the moment, and that may be, perhaps, more style than substance.

Donald: Also, people tend to think in genres now. I notice younger musicians will say: *It's a little like this and a little like that with some trip hop mixed in.* Even though it does have certain elements from jazz, and so on, we don't really think of it as a genre of any kind. It's just what we like.

Walter: Basically, we're trying to make harmonically interesting music.

Donald: More or less unknown.

Walter: Yeah, that in and of itself puts us way out in left field.

Gaslighting Abbie

Words and Music by
Walter Becker and Donald Fagen

Moderately

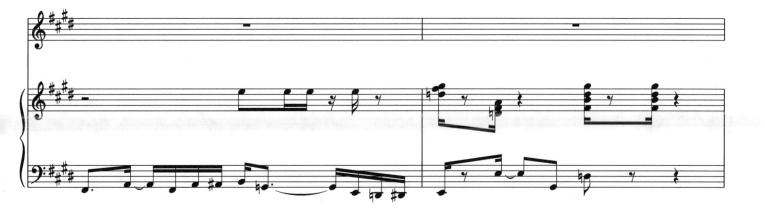

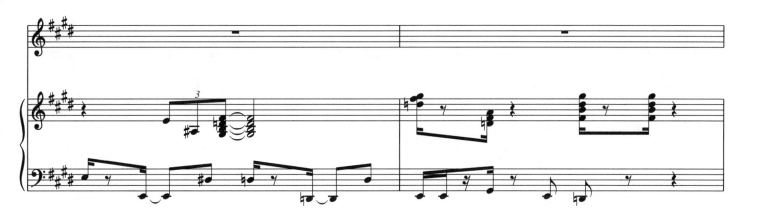

%

E9

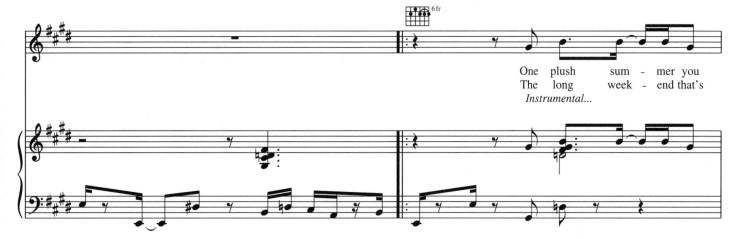

One plush sum - mer you
The long week - end that's
Instrumental...

come to me _____ ripe and read - y   and bad through and through, __
com-ing up fast, _____ let's get bus - y.   There's just too much __ to do. _____

with that deep, mys - ti - cal
That black min - i looks

soul syn - er - gy ____ pump - ing stead - y
just like the one ____ she's been miss - in'.

be - tween me and you.
Feels good on you.

Lov - in' all the beau - ti - ful
There's a few i - tems we

work we've done, ____ *car - a mi - a,*
need in town, ____ *al - lez vous,* girl.

and it's bare - ly ____ Ju - ly. ____
There's no time _ to waste, _

If we keep on bop-pin' un -
such as fresh ca - ble and

til La - bor Day, ___ lit - tle miz Ab - bie, bye bye.
fif - teen - watt bulbs, ___ cou - ple doz - en. It's a big old place.

...Instrumental ends

What will it be? Some sooth-ing herb tea ___
Let's keep it light. We'll do a fright night ___
How can you knock this might - y spite - lock? ___

___ might be just the thing. ___ Let's say we spike it with De - lu - din. Or else
___ with blood and ev - 'ry - thing. ___ Some punk - y laugh-ter from the kitch - en. And then,
___ Check out the work it - self. ___ A mix of el - e - gance and func - tion. That's right,

may - be to-night a hand of sol - i - taire. __
a nice, re - lax - ing hand of sol - i - taire. __
a tweak or two and then she's out of __ here. __

Flame is __ the game, __

the game we __ call gas - light-ing ab - bie. It's a

lus - cious __ in - ven - tion __ for three. One sum-mer by __ the sea. __

You can choose __ the mu -

D.S. al Coda

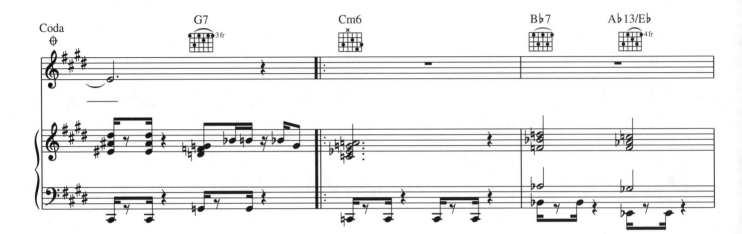

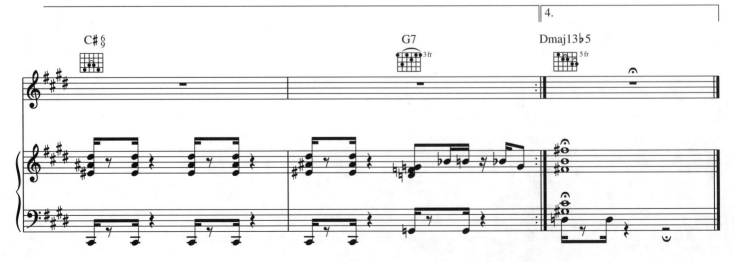

16

What a Shame About Me

Words and Music by
Walter Becker and Donald Fagen

2.

D7sus4

I was grind - ing through my day ___ gig, stack - in'
"Talk to me; ___ do you ev - er see an - y -
both ran out ___ of small ___ talk. The con -

cut - outs at ___ the Strand, ___ when in walks Fran - ny from
bod - y else from our old crew?" ___ Bob- by Da - kine ___ won the
nec - tion seemed ___ to go dead. I was a - bout to say, ___ "Hey,

N. Y. U. ___ We were quite an i - tem back then.
Bun - sen Prize. ___ He's com - ing out with some - thing new.
have a nice life." ___ She touched my hand ___ and said, ___

G7sus4

Talked a - bout her films and shows ___ and C - D's. Don't know what else. ___
Al - an owns a chain of Steam - er Heav - ens. Bar - ry is the soft - ware king. ___
"I just had ___ this great ___ i - dea. This could be ver - y cool. ___

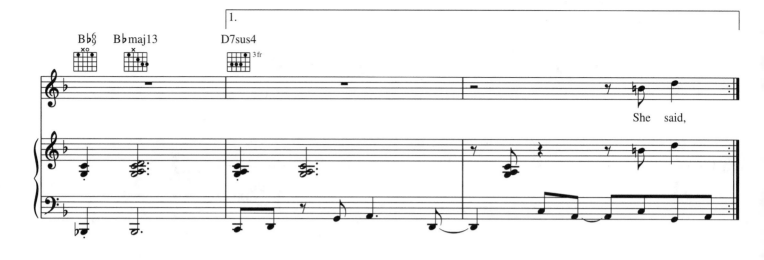

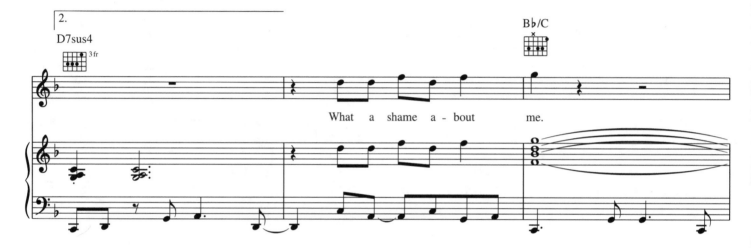

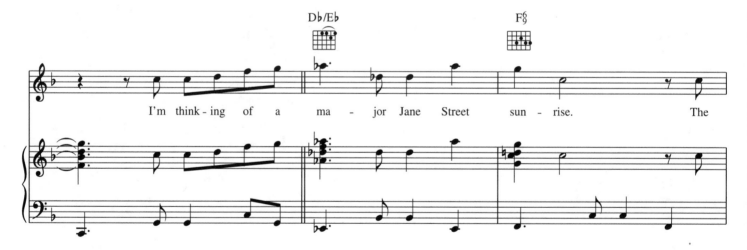

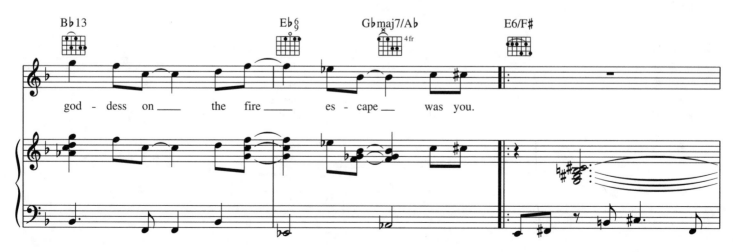

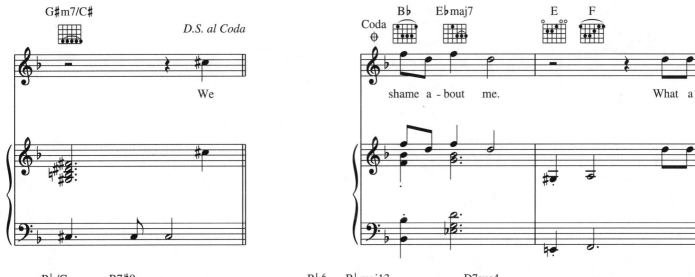

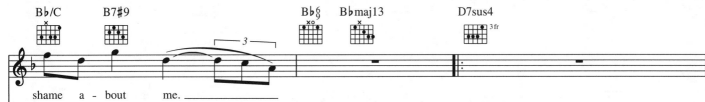

Repeat and fade

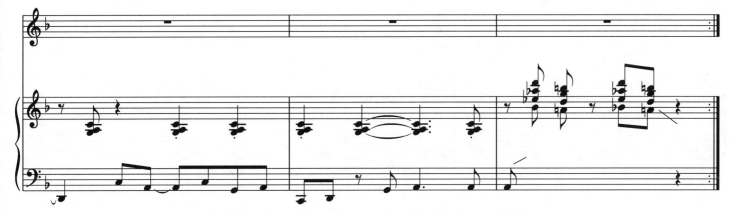

Two Against Nature

Words and Music by
Walter Becker and Donald Fagen

that whole crew. 'Cross the lob - by the wick - er wind chair flew.
worse than that. Pan - a - tel - la and old black der - by hat.
Jer - ry Gar - ry, sprin-kling chick - en wa-ter, gon - na hush all three.

All the nice peo - ple, good - ly souls, quak - ing in __ their res - pec - tive
Call your doc - tor, call your shrink. West - ern sci - ence, she strict - ly
Beau-ti - ful house - wife in deep dis - tress. 'Spe - c'lly you _____ de - serve the

hid - ey - holes. Ev - 'ry-one's wast - ed in this grue - some dream.
rink - y - dink. They all ma - si - ssi but we hang tough.
ver - y best. Two a-gainst na - ture, they got that stuff.

Em7

Not a one __ of them left to hear you scream. Two a-gainst na - ture, don't you
Ap - sa - tive - ly gon-na help you beat that stuff. Two a-gainst na - ture, tan and
Good things hap - pen-ing when you see a - bout us. Two a-gainst na - ture, love this

mf

know. Who's gon - na grok the shape __ of things to go? Two a-gainst na - ture, make them
lean. Put - tin' big heat on skank - y things un - seen. Two a-gainst na - ture, sling-ing
gig. Pull up the weeds be - fore __ they're too damn big. Two a-gainst na - ture, stand a -

1.

To Coda ⊕

groan. Who's gon - na break the shape _____ of things un - known? Things un -
dread. These boys wan - na bang the skulls _____ of things un -
lone. Who's gon - na chase the shape _____ of things un -

A♭7♯9

known.

mp

2.

Am9(maj7)   E7/A

dead.

2nd time, D.S. al Coda

Coda

known?

Two a-gainst na - ture, don't you know. Who's gon - na drop the boom _ on things to go?

Two a-gainst na - ture, make them groan. Gon-na go bang-zoom to the moon on things un - known.

Scrape the wall - boards, the whole damn batch.

Catch the mag - got - y eggs be - fore they hatch. Pep-per and rat - bone

make damn sure. Shake the rub - bish out on the pat - i - o floor.

Soak the tim - ber ___ with spe - cial spray. Nuke the it - ty bit - ty ones right

where they lay. Whip the bas - tards while they still green.

Take the fire - mop; sweep it kiss-ing clean.

Ab7#9

Repeat and fade

Janie Runaway

Words and Music by
Walter Becker and Donald Fagen

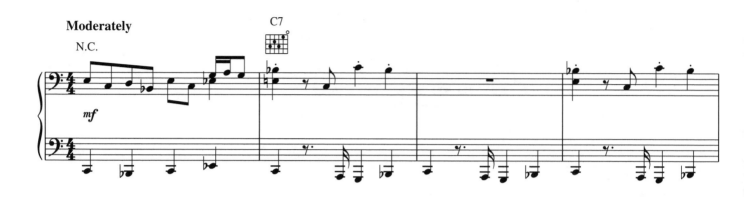

It must have been my luck-y Thurs-day
Let's grab some take-out from Dean and De-Lu-ca,
Let's plan a week-end a-lone to-geth-er,

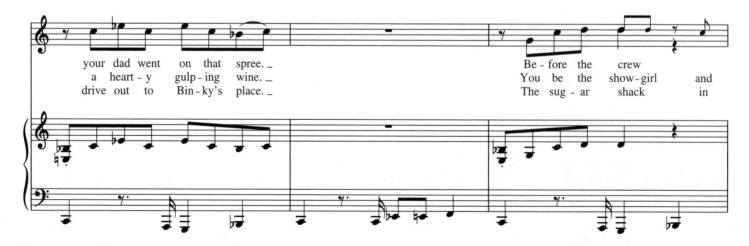

your dad went on that spree. _
a heart-y gulp-ing wine. _
drive out to Bin-ky's place. _

Be-fore the crew
You be the show-girl and
The sug-ar shack in

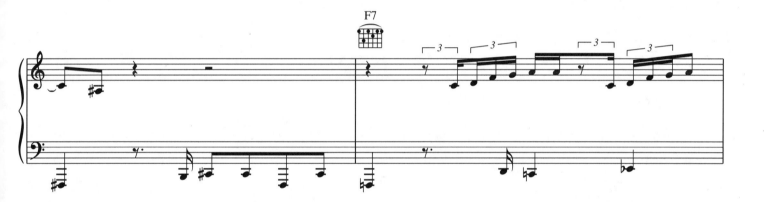

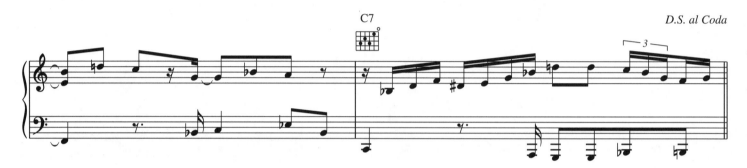

Run-a-way.

Who _ makes the morn - ing fab - u - lous, _

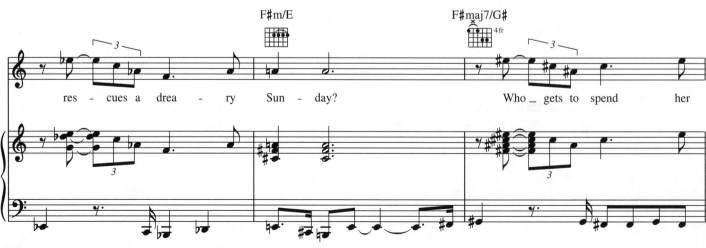

res - cues a drea - ry Sun - day?

Who _ gets to spend her

Almost Gothic

Words and Music by
Walter Becker and Donald Fagen

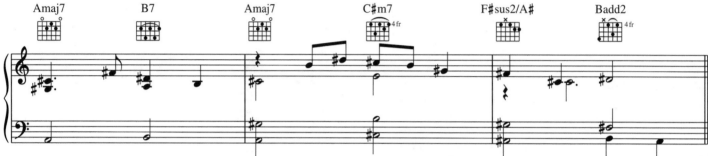

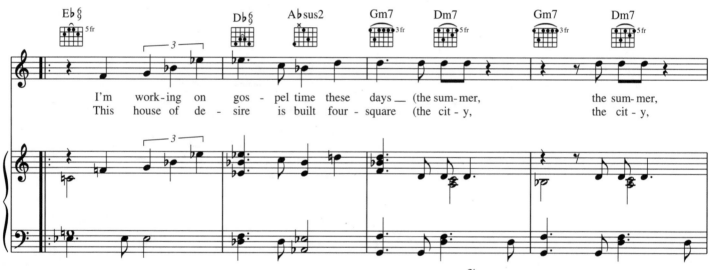

I'm work-ing on gos - pel time these days __ (the sum-mer, the sum-mer,
This house of de - sire is built four-square (the cit - y, the cit - y,

this could be the cool ___ part of the sum-mer).
the clean - est kit - ten in the cit - y).

The sloe-eyed crea-ture in the
When she speaks it's like the
I'm pret-ty sure that what she's

34

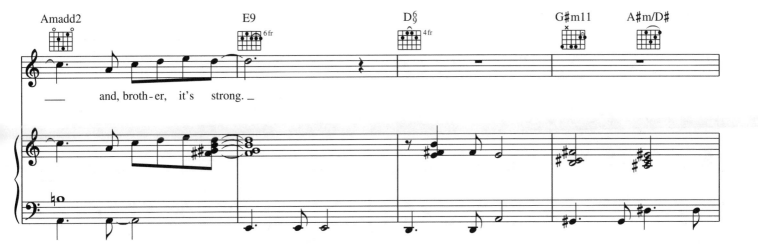

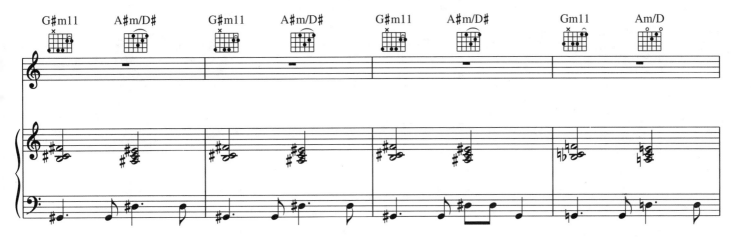

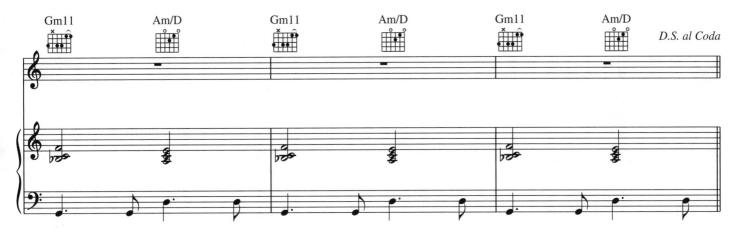

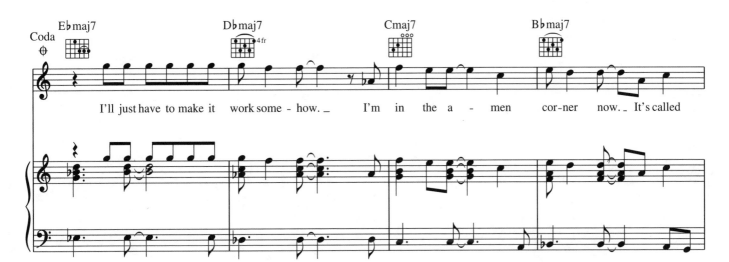

Jack of Speed

Words and Music by
Walter Becker and Donald Fagen

Moderately slow

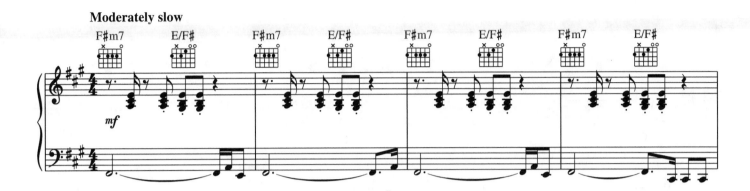

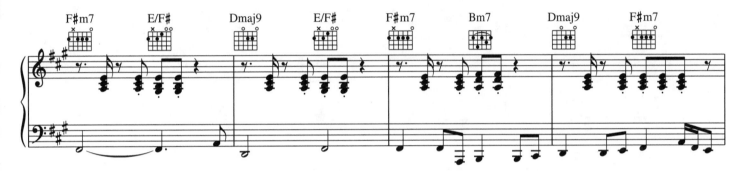

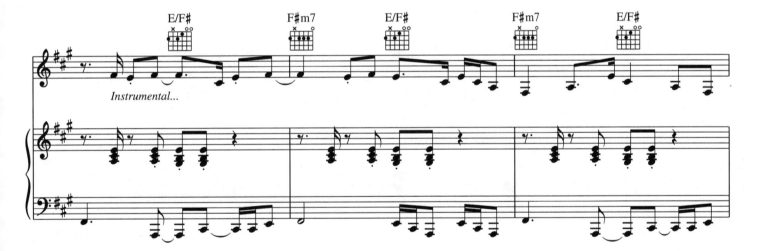

40

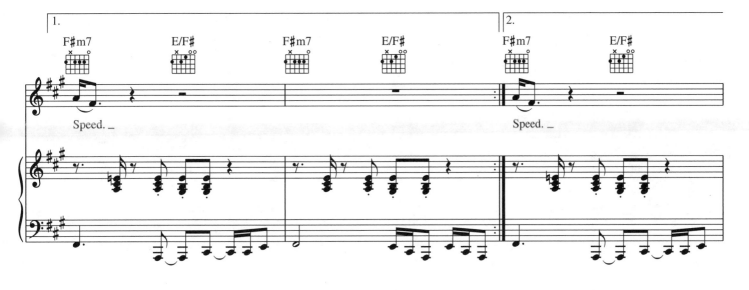

Speed. _

Speed. _

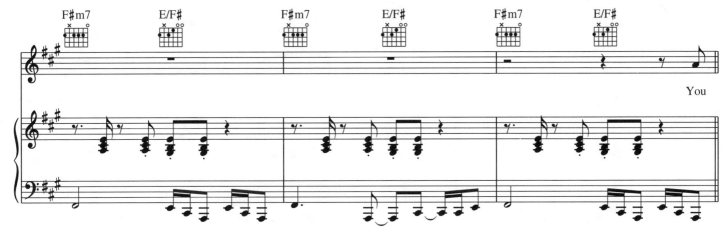

You

may - be got luck-y ___ for a few good _ years. _ There's no way _ back from

there to __ here. He's a one - way _ rid-er ___ on the shriek ex - press, _ and his

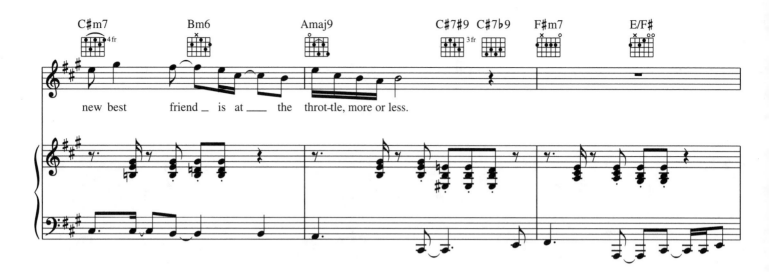

new best friend __ is at __ the throt-tle, more or less.

D.S. al Coda

Coda

Speed.__ *Instrumental...*

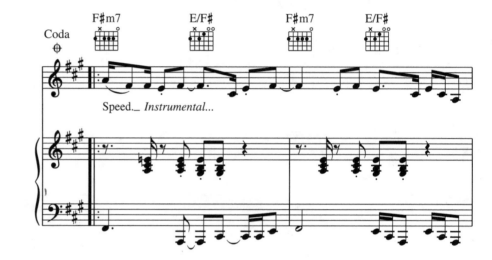

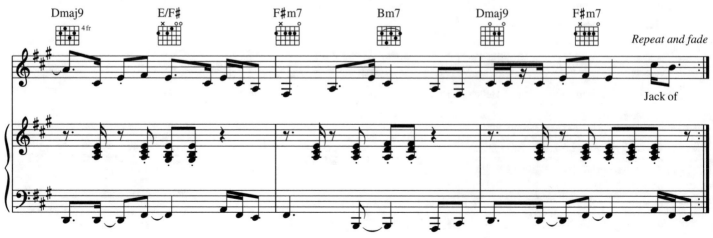

Repeat and fade

Jack of

42

Cousin Dupree

Words and Music by
Walter Becker and Donald Fagen

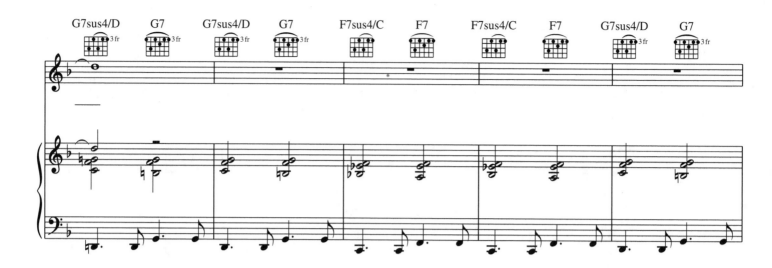

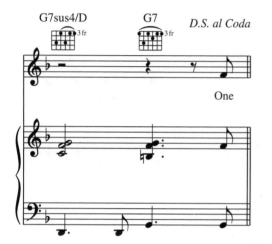 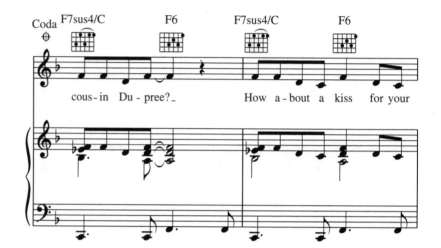

One

cous - in Du - pree? __   How a - bout a kiss   for your

cous - in Du - pree? __   How a - bout a kiss   for your cous - in Du - pree? __

Repeat and fade

How __ a-bout a kiss   for your cous-in Du - pree? __

Negative Girl

Words and Music by
Walter Becker and Donald Fagen

Moderately

She's lost, she's late. She's zoom-ing on a couch some - where.
skin, like milk. It's like she's nev - er seen the sun.
on the train to some-where up by Ford - ham Road.

An-oth-er neg-a-tive girl at the edge of ___ the
An-oth-er neg-a-tive girl spin-ning out of ___ the

frame. De-li-cious-ly tox-ic. The o-rig-i-nal clas-sic thing.
frame. Ex-quis-ite-ly lim-pid. The o-rig-i-nal clas-sic thing.

More of the same.
More of the same.

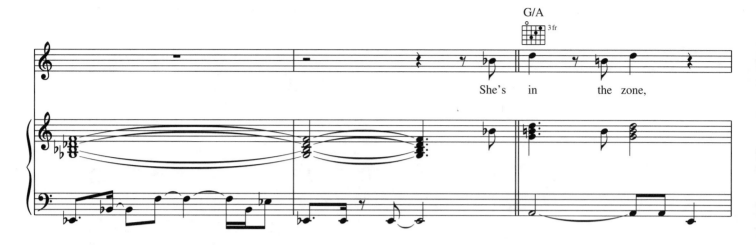

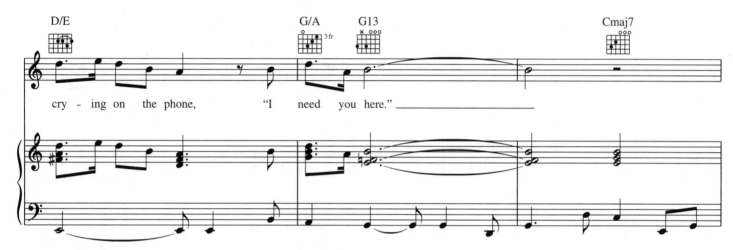

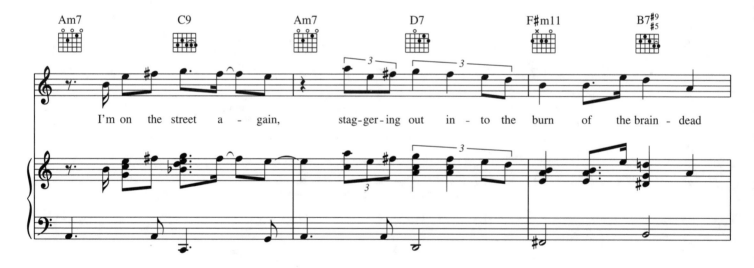

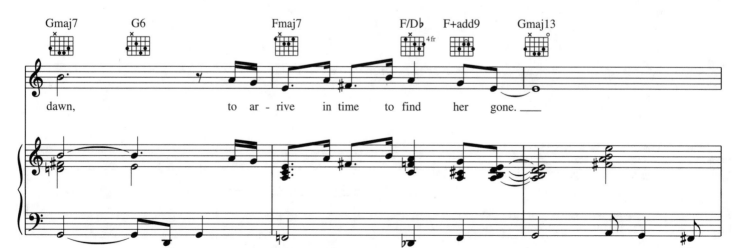

She's

A goof, a buzz, if

that is what it was. Then how do you ex - plain ___

the way she looks when _ she's drag-ging me out to dance with her in the sum - mer rain? _

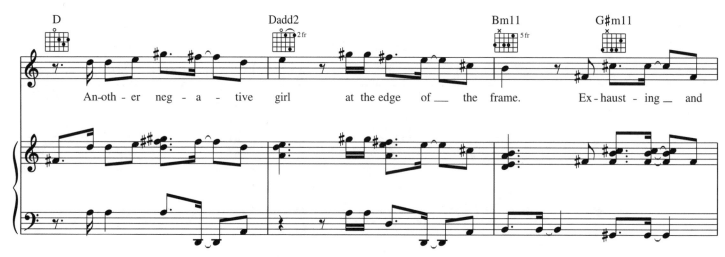

Another negative girl at the edge of __ the frame. Exhausting __ and

luscious. The original classic thing. More of the same, more of the

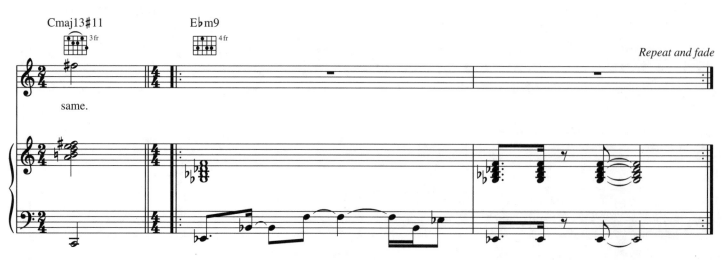

same.

West of Hollywood

Words and Music by
Walter Becker and Donald Fagen

Moderately fast

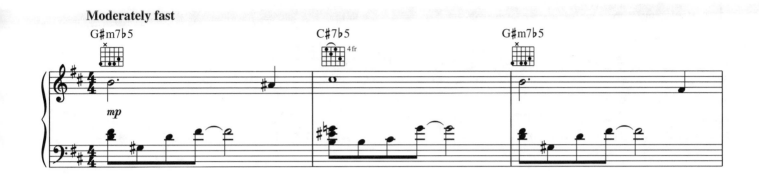

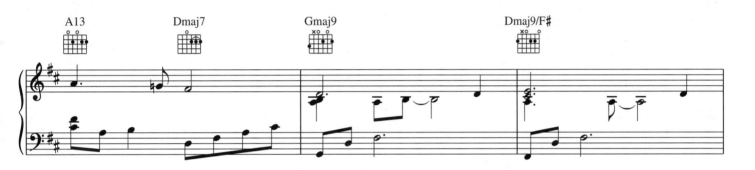

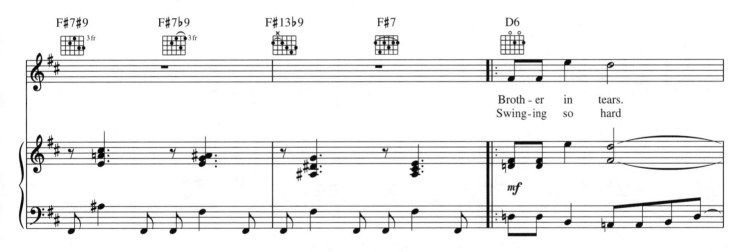

Broth - er in tears.
Swing-ing so hard

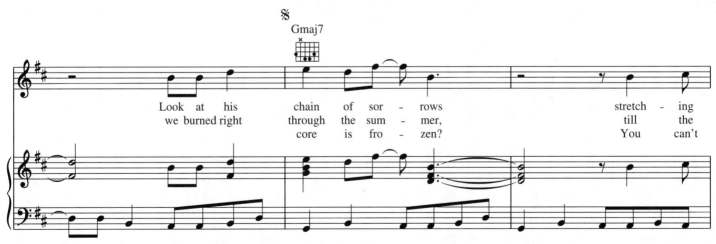

Look at his chain of sor - rows stretch - ing
we burned right through the sum - mer, till the
core is fro - zen? You can't

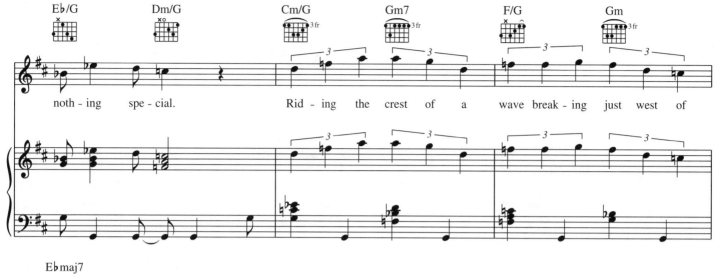

noth - ing spe - cial. Rid - ing the crest of a wave break - ing just west of

Hol - ly - wood. _

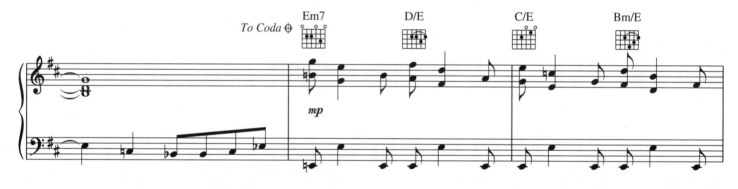

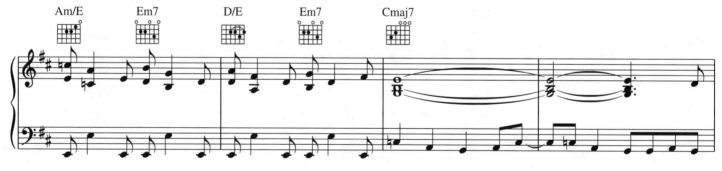

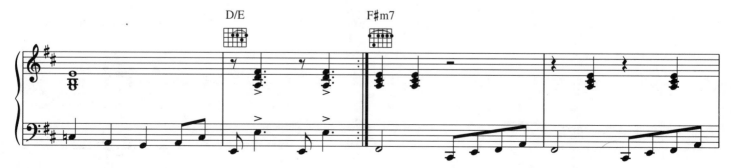

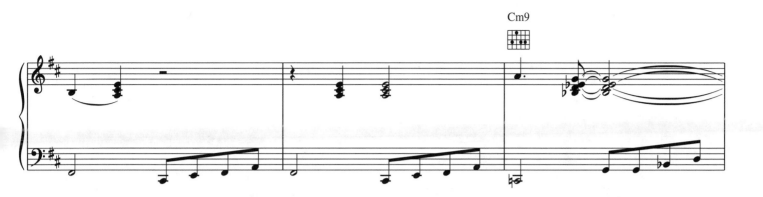

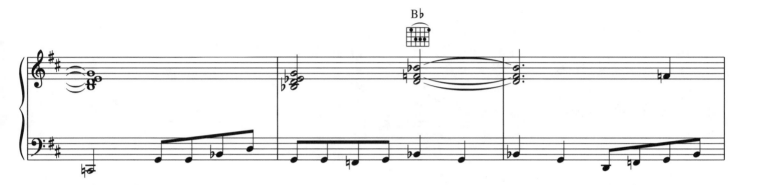

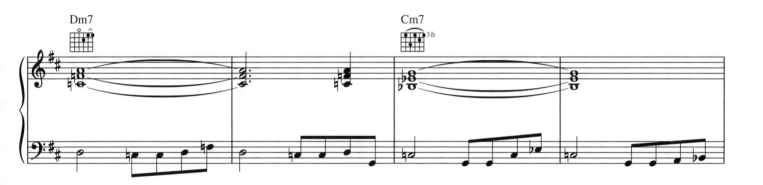

She reached out ____ for my hand while I watched my - self lurch a -

cross the room. __ And I al-most got ____ there, I al-most got __

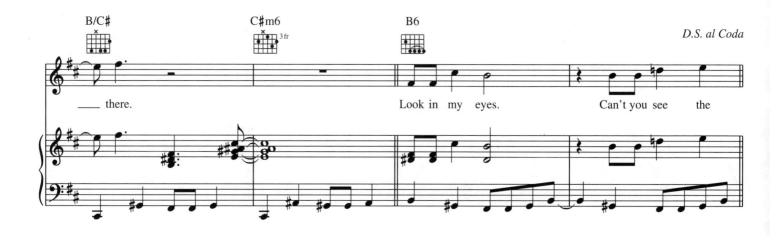

__ there. Look in my eyes. Can't you see the

I'm way deep __ in - to noth-ing spe - cial. _____

(Sing 1st time only)

58

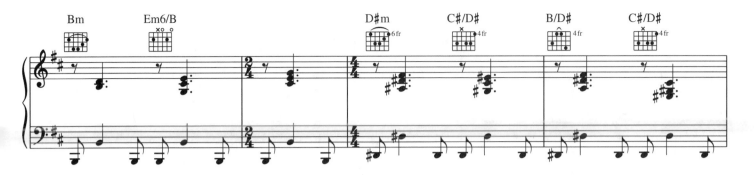

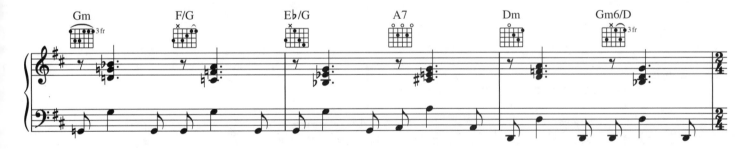

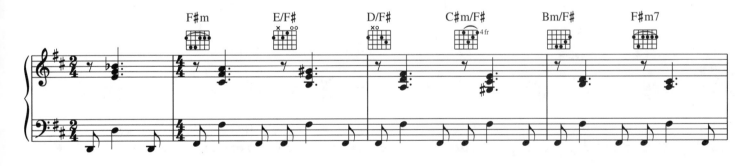

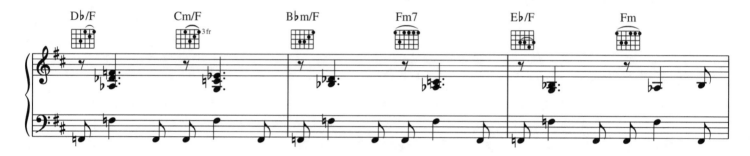

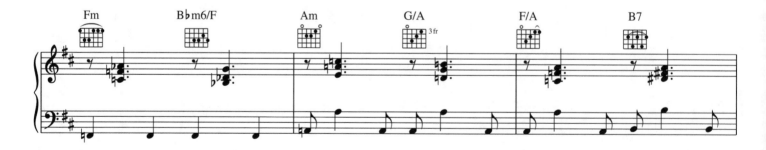

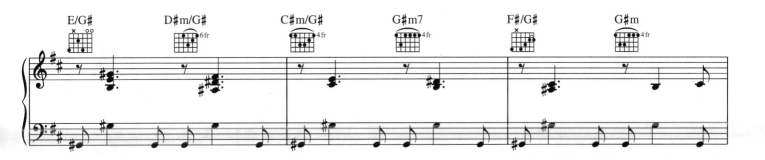

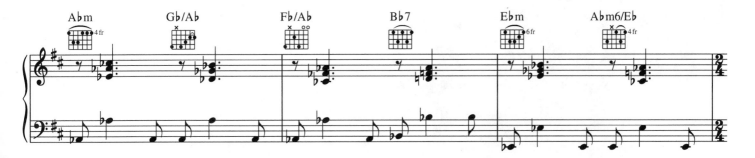

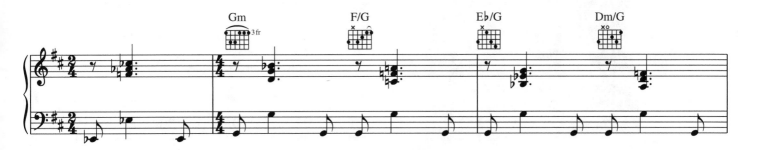

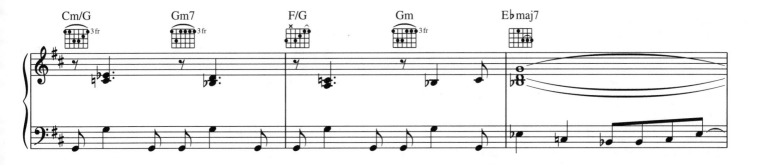

Repeat and fade

GREAT STEELY DAN
BOOKS

STEELY DAN'S GREATEST SONGS
15 more trademark Steely Dan songs, including: Aja • Chain Lightning • Daddy Don't Live in That New York City No More • Everyone's Gone to the Movies • Haitian Divorce • Josie • Pretzel Logic • Reeling in the Years • and more.
02500168 Play-It-Like-It-Is Guitar $19.95

BEST OF STEELY DAN FOR SOLO GUITAR
11 great solos, including: Aja • Babylon Sisters • Deacon Blues • Doctor Wu • Gaucho • Haitian Divorce • Hey Nineteen • Kid Charlemagne • Peg • Rikki Don't Lose That Number • Third World Man.
02500169 Solo Guitar...$12.95

BEST OF STEELY DAN FOR DRUMS
10 classic songs for drums from Steely Dan. Includes: Aja • Babylon Sisters • The Faz • Peg • Two Against Nature • Time Out of Mind • What a Shame About Me • and more.
02500312 Drums $18.95

STEELY DAN LEGENDARY LICKS (GUITAR)
28 extensive musical examples from: Aja • Babylon Sisters • Black Cow • Bodhisattva • Josie • Kid Charlemagne • Parker's Band • Peg • Reeling in the Years • Rikki Don't Lose That Number • and many more.
02500160 Guitar Book/CD Pack...$19.95

STEELY DAN JUST THE RIFFS FOR GUITAR
by Rich Zurkowski
More than 40 hot licks from Steely Dan. Includes: Babylon Sisters • Black Friday • The Boston Rag • Deacon Blues • Kid Charlemagne • King of the World • Peg • Reeling in the Years • Rikki Don't Lose That Number • Sign in Stranger • and more.
02500159 Just the Riffs – Guitar..$19.95

THE ART OF STEELY DAN (KEYBOARD)
Features over 30 great Steely Dan tunes for piano: Aja • Black Cow • Bodhisattva • Hey Nineteen • I.G.Y. (What a Beautiful World) • Parker's Band • Reeling in the Years • Third World Man • Your Gold Teeth II • many more.
02500171 Piano Solo $19.95

STEELY DAN JUST THE RIFFS FOR KEYBOARD
28 keyboard riffs, including: Babylon Sisters • The Boston Rag • Deacon Blues • Don't Take Me Alive • Green Earrings • Hey Nineteen • Peg • Reeling in the Years • Rikki Don't Lose That Number • and more.
02500164 Just the Riffs – Keyboard $9.95

Prices, contents, and availability subject to change without notice.

BEST OF STEELY DAN
A fantastic collection of 15 hits showcasing the sophisticated sounds of Steely Dan. Includes: Babylon Sisters • Bad Sneakers • Deacon Blues • Do It Again • FM • Here at the Western World • Hey Nineteen • I.G.Y. (What a Beautiful World) • Josie • Kid Charlemagne • My Old School • Peg • Reeling in the Years • Rikki Don't Lose That Number • Time out of Mind.
02500165 Piano/Vocal/Guitar $14.95

STEELY DAN – ANTHOLOGY
A comprehensive collection of 30 of their biggest hits, including: Aja • Big Noise, New York • Black Cow • Black Friday • Bodhisattva • Deacon Blues • Do It Again • Everyone's Gone to the Movies • FM • Gaucho • Hey Nineteen • Josie • Reeling in the Years • more!
02500166 Piano/Vocal/Guitar $17.95

BEST OF STEELY DAN FOR GUITAR
15 transcriptions of Steely Dan's jazz/rock tunes, including: Bad Sneakers • Black Friday • The Boston Rag • Deacon Blues • FM • Green Earrings • Kid Charlemagne • Parker's Band • Peg • Rikki Don't Lose That Number • Third World Man • Time Out of Mind • and more.
02500167 Play-It-Like-It-Is Guitar $19.95

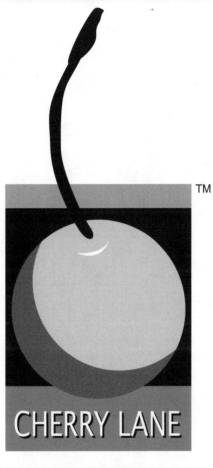

CHERRY LANE

MUSIC COMPANY

QUALITY IN PRINTED MUSIC